SMARTYpants
secrets

STRESS

It's a Real KILLER – of Health, Happiness, Life - It's a Serious Condition, So Stop Taking it Lightly

D.R. Martin, PhD*

(*Personal human Development)

Smartypants Press
Falmouth, Maine 04105
www.SmartyPantsSecrets.com

ISBN 13: 978-1-943971-14-5
ISBN 10: 1943971145

The SmartyPants Secrets Concept

A **SmartyPants Secret** is that **one piece of information** that you need to know to make every job a little bit, or maybe a lot, **easier**. Almost everything we do in life has a SmartyPants secret that to it, that knowing the "secret" would help tremendously in shortening the learning curve.

After experiencing many "a ha!" moments that were previous head bangers, I realized that there was a lot of grief – i.e. aggravation, wasted time, spent resources - that could have been saved if I had known to tap into the insider information that others had and I was lacking. A SmartyPants secret is that crucial bit of timely knowledge.

We all want a magic bullet answer that solves all of our problems in one fell swoop and makes everything go perfectly well, preferably in record time! We want that magic to happen right NOW, to be easily done, and to be preferably cheap, or at least not at great expense. There are a lot of demands on our unattainable magic ☺

For example, one day I looked at my face and damn if I didn't see a "sun spot" (nastily also called a "liver" spot) marring the surface of my otherwise smooth face on the right lower cheek. I scheduled an appointment at the dermatologist to verify the find and see if it could be lasered off. She sent me to an aesthetician who gave me some key information that made a huge difference in my decision of what to do next.

I was told that my even slightly darker (Asian) skin carries more pigment than Caucasian skin obviously. But what's not obvious is the way the body works, specifically the way the skin works, which is that when you wound the skin's surface, which laser surgery would certainly do, extra pigments rush to the spot to heal it (the "job" of pigment is to protect the underlying cells). The net result is that non-Caucasian skin heals into darker scabs and scars. (I have noticed this phenomena before but never made a direct connection.) Why then would I ever choose to have laser surgery on my face to remove a mark only to end up with an even darker mark? Yikes!

Obviously I wouldn't, but without this specialized knowledge about different results with different skin types, that even the dermatologist didn't know (yes, she was the recommender of the laser surgery option) I would've made a poor decision, with permanent negative results. A SmartyPants timely secret to the rescue!

Experts, who have hours of experience doing what the newbie is attempting to do, have expert knowledge, which may not be so secret, but it is **key information** that the novice greatly needs.

If you've ever struggled with something then learned the 'something' afterwards that caused you to say to yourself or to say aloud, "*Well, **if I only known THAT before I did this**, it would've made a world of difference!*" then you just learned a SmartyPants secret - the hard way.

The short SmartyPants Secrets books give you the secret that you need on a given topic, the most important piece of information that makes the greatest difference between easier success and hard-fought failure.

When I was young there was a professor at Cornell University, which in his obituary listed him as "***the last man to know everything***." I was taken by the concept of anyone knowing everything there is to know contained in one brain. Oh, to have such a mind!

But **to know everything**, logical facts and figures, and **to be able to do everything** are **two different things**. Brain power doesn't equal skill and expertise.

Today that one brain that knows everything is the Internet. There is so much information today available on the Internet; we can all be like that professor at Cornell and have access to all knowledge at the click of our fingertips.

More knowledge than we could ever consume - **who has time** to go through it all? Most of the time **what you really want is to know is the crux of the subject** on hand, not the whole litany of everything imaginable that is available to know.

Tell me just what I need to know! (and I likely don't know what specific knowledge to ask for). It's literally impossible to know what you don't know. Let the expertise of knowledgeable others guide you.

If you are new to a topic the **SmartyPants secret can save you time and effort**, which are important to your success. Not a complete course on the topic, which you can certainly get elsewhere, the SmartyPants secrets concept is primarily to help you **not miss the key information needed for success**.

The building block of knowledge that the foundation rests upon; the Keystone or cornerstone knowledge makes a critical difference, especially when that knowledge that you do have, or think you have, is **faulty, incomplete or missing** entirely.

The concept of **social proof** states that when we have no prior experience in a given situation we rely on **others to show us the way**. We believe that lacking personal knowledge, that their situation is similar to our situation, and therefore what worked for them has a high probability of working for us.

We quiz others about our shared circumstances around the situation to verify that their solution is a good one. Plus, we think: *there's nothing to lose in trying since I don't have a better answer.*

Then when what worked for another doesn't happen to work for us, we are reminded that **we are all different people**, with different variables that impact success or failure. Some solutions to problems are hit or miss depending on who we are. And sometimes success depends on having and following the right key knowledge.

Solving problems is not the complete SmartyPants concept, although SmartyPants secrets can indeed offer real help for real problems. Rather the full concept is that having that key knowledge piece makes efforts easier and successful quicker; hopefully **avoiding having the problem in the first place.** We do anything in life because we have a goal to achieve. Reaching that goal successfully, quickly and easier than without knowing the SmartPants secret is the SmartyPants concept.

And because **all SmartyPants secrets have a physiological root**, grounded in our shared human biology, every SmartyPants secret is valid for everyone, no matter who you are. While we are all uniquely different from each other, we have a **common biology** consisting of inherited traits that stretch back to the Neanderthal era.

Applying a SmartyPants secret **will work for you no matter who you are**. And in our busy world, who doesn't want to save time and know the SmartyPants secret to anything?

Why ever risk hindering easier success by not knowing the core success secret?

STRESS

So Much to DO!
So Many Deadlines!
So Little Time for All the Demands!
SO, MAKE A CHANGE!

The Nike logo *Just Do It!* would be good advice for all the stressed out people, who are absolutely killing themselves with an unhealthy work load, too little sleep, being pulled in too many directions. **Is this you?**

The kids are young and demanding. Work is at a critical point (but work is *always* that way). The parents depend on you and they (and you) aren't getting any younger.

Life moves at a rapid pace, and somehow you believe it all hinges on you – you simply can't disappoint. Everyone NEEDS you to deliver, and you always do. Until the day you don't, which may be coming sooner than you think...

STRESS RELIEVER

Bang
Head
Here

Directions:
1. Place on a firm surface
2. Follow instructions in circle
3. Repeat step 2 until stress diminishes or you are unconscious
4. If unconscious, cease stress reduction activity

You have so much responsibility hanging on your broad shoulders, or perhaps your sagging shoulders these days. Without you killing yourself, the world as you know it would surely fall apart.

But what are you really doing to that body under those sore and tired shoulders with all the stress you are carrying around without relief?

You just can't seem to be able to relax – not on vacation, when you should be unwinding. Not at night, when you should be resting. Not ever, really, which is doing steady physiological internal damage.

Your eating is out of control, as you stress-eat to feel better and are gaining too much weight. Or the opposite – losing weight due to high stress and lack of appetite.

Stress can cause hair loss, alopecia – defined as an immune system irregularity that triggers sudden loss of hair that may or may not ever regrow.

My 20-something daughter experienced this when she moved to the West Coast with a boyfriend, who then left. Her health and hair suffered as she stressed about finances, her living conditions, and the state of her love life.

If a child was crying, we would stop to soothe. If a friend was upset, we would tend to them. But when it comes to our own internal tears and screaming, we look away, ignore, dismiss as nothing important. Listening to your body is an important part of health.

What stress symptoms are you choosing to ignore?

Just do it –decide to make a change to reduce stress!

EITHER EAT OR BE EATEN

By Frits Ahlefeldt

A good definition of stress is: *Someone is intent on eating you, or vice versa*.

The PBS series "Hunt" is a good example of the predator and prey situation with the animal's very lives and the lives of their young are at stake daily. Most animals spend most of their waking hours just **trying to survive**. Survival dictates finding their next meal or avoiding becoming somebody else's dinner.

There is a reoccurring bird visitor to our front porch every year with the female building a nest and carefully laying and hatching five eggs twice each summer. Of those 10 young hatchlings, some are pushed out of the nest because they are weak, some are not fed because there's not enough food to go around, and of the ones that make it through infancy and fly way, only one in four will make it to full adulthood. Stressful lives in nature are commonplace.

In the world of humans the effects of stress are internal, **eating away at us from within**. Sadly, we are really doing the harm to ourselves, because we don't recognize the dangers of stress, or know how to handle and control it properly.

WE ARE STRESSED OUT!

➢ Unrealistic deadlines, and we're always running behind!

➢ Unforgiving bosses, damn him for always catching your errors and seeming to overlook all the good that you do!

➢ Holy, god - that commute! Out of (our) control traffic raises our stress levels daily.

The US ranks as the fifth highest country in stress levels, with ***39% of citizens report experiencing stress on a regular basis.**

Not surprisingly, **college graduates** report feeling more stressed than non-graduates.

Two thirds of people surveyed report that their **work** has a significant impact on their stress levels.

Employers report that **health-care expenses are 50% higher for employees** who reports feeling high levels of stress.

(*GHWBI data, 2008/2009)

39% are

stressed

A Few of Life's Many STRESSORS

- **Too many choices!** (as described in the 1970 book *Future Shock*, with technology creating information overload – pretty accurate then, and certainly now, 46 years later TMI overwhelms daily)

- **Crowding!** (anxiety up, stress chemicals rise, immune system sags, too many people in too tight spaces, arghhhh)

- **Feeling bad about yourself!** (we love ourselves, except when we don't...and that low self-esteem is a killer in a society that values high confidence)

- **Performance reviews**! (of course you're doing a good job at work, but review time causes employee defensiveness and stressors as the boss seemingly loves to exert power and subordination)

- **Long lines!** (you always seem to pick the slowest moving line, with things moving at a snail's pace, and no apparent discernible reason for the delay...why is the line you pick always the slow one?)

- **People not following the rules!** (the cheats in life who always seem to get away with it – no fair to us rule-following good guys)

- **Traffic!** (no additional comment needed – traffic congestion = stress!!!)

Biological Evolution of Stress

We have the **same internal system today as humans had 25,000 years ago**. When faced with threats, stress was the body's survival mechanism, allowing rational thinking to be abandoned for a faster response.

Saber tooth tiger roaring your way? Should you fight (only if you had a weapon on hand and a death wish) or freeze (lie down and play dead and hope that the beast is blind and can't smell the fear reeking from all of your pores) or flee (the likely response, how fast can you get that blood pumping to those legs to move you the heck out of there!)

In today's world the saber tooth tigers are gone but the stress response remains. The adrenaline flows in the body gearing for fight or flight or freeze in panic, when faced with the daily mental stressors brought on by, not wild animals hungry for dinner, but "wild" situations or other people hungry for a verbal/ego fight.

Back when stress was a savior, when the stressor went away, so did the accompanying stress. Adrenaline levels dropped down to normal and didn't remain a damaging constant, as often is the case today.

The condition of being chronically stressed is prevalent for many people, the adrenaline rarely getting a chance to subside. Maintaining high levels of adrenaline over long periods of time is harmful to the body, causing wear and tear on our biological regulatory systems.

Some people love the adrenaline rush and stress, participating in challenging and ultra-challenging physical events. To accomplish a physical feat with the new addition of a high danger element is really upping the ante.

The running of the bulls in Spain used to be a great thrill, still is for many. For others it's too calm, opting instead for events like marathons with Africa's Big 5 – running with the potential of a charging rhino, leopard, buffalo, or lion delivers an inimitable thrill.

But for most**, stress, the once savior of Neanderthals, is today a tyrant** (to the chronically stressed) and a plague (to the merely routinely stressed).

The Stress Hormone: ADRENALINE or NOREPINEPHRINE

Adrenaline is mainly responsible for the immediate arousal reactions of stress to escape imminent 'death'. Yikes! - the hypothalamus senses the danger and sends a strong and immediate signal to the adrenal glands that a dire threat is nearby. Within seconds, drastic changes occur:

Heart pounds (pumps 2 to 3 times the normal speed to send nutrient-rich blood to the major muscles in the extremities)
Muscles tense (ready to either run fast or hit hard)
Blood pressure soars (capillaries close down so the body can survive a surface wound and not bleed out)
Breathing quickens (delivering maximum oxygen to the brain and muscles)
Pupils dilate (to better see the danger)
Anticipatory sweating (overworked sympathetic nervous system is ramped up)
Excess waste elimination (drop any useless waste to make you light on your feet)

Adrenaline also delivers an *energy surge*, and strong *attention focus*, so within seconds your body is supercharged to run, hit, see, hear, think, and jump higher, to help you avoid near certain death! Only today's stressors are hardly life-threatening. But the effects of chronic stress can be.

To make modern matters worse, **caffeine** triggers the release of adrenaline. The combination of the two puts the body into a hyper-aroused state of stress, allowing emotions to rule behavior, with a long duration of effect due to caffeine's long half-life. The body was built for short bursts of intermittent adrenaline rushes; it is not meant to sustain prolonged periods of stress.

Norepinephrine is released from the adrenal glands and from the brain, as a backup to adrenaline, should the adrenal glands fail. Its role is to help shift blood away from nonessential areas, like the skin (causing blood pressure to soar) and the brain (so logical thinking is diminished), to more essential areas needed to fight or flee, like the major muscles in the legs and arms.

Depending on the long-term stressor's impact and on the personal disposition of the person on handling stress, it can take *from 30 minutes to several days for the body to return to normal* when overtaxed by stress.

The Stress Hormone: CORTISOL, and Adrenal Fatigue

Cortisol is a steroid hormone produced by the adrenal glands. Its function is to influence, regulate or modulate many bodily functions that occur in response to stress, including:

- Blood sugar (glucose) levels
- Fat, protein and carbohydrate metabolism to maintain blood glucose
- Immune responses
- Blood pressure
- Heart and blood vessel contraction
- Central nervous system activation
- Canker sores (appearing before a big event are indicative of the presence of elevated cortisol levels)

Cortisol levels fluctuate throughout the day and night in a circadian rhythm that peaks around 8am, dropping to its lowest point around 4am. It is vital to health for the adrenals to release more cortisol in response to stress. It is also **very important that bodily functions and cortisol levels return to normal after a stressful event has ended.**

Unfortunately, **in our high-stress culture, the stress response is activated so frequently that the body does not always have a chance to return to normal**. This can lead to health problems from either <u>too much secreted cortisol</u> or <u>too little cortisol</u> – adrenal fatigue – resulting in debilitating chronic stress.

or

(*PSTD is a condition where the hippocampus shuts down under intense stress, causing inappropriate or out of context responses/behavior.)

STRESS SYMPTOMS

Watch for these signs that you getting stressed and maybe you don't even know it, *yet* – before it's too late and the internal damage is already happening!

- ❖ **Frequent headaches** (hitting the bottle of aspirin/ibuprofen often?)

- ❖ **Fatigue** (drinking a lot of coffee to try and stay awake?)

- ❖ **Back pain** (caused by tensing muscles for long periods of time)

- ❖ **Nausea, upset stomach** (*stress can literally gnaw away at you)

- ❖ **Change in appetite** (sudden change in eating habits; stress overeating)

- ❖ **Frequent colds or bouts of flu** (weakened immune system)

- ❖ **Excessive sweating** (not just nervousness, also from routine stress)

- ❖ **Loss/diminished sex drive** (work stress hurts overall happiness)

- ❖ **Irritability** (snapping at others and being generally disagreeable)

- ❖ **Nervousness** (jumpy at the littlest things?)

*During an especially stressful time in my early working career, I was feeling neglected stress symptoms regularly, that became worse as time went on. It finally got to the point that when I would wake up in the morning, I felt fine after the restorative sleep the night brought. But the minute my feet landed on the floor and I got out of bed to get dressed, I could feel the stress starting in my stomach. It felt like a ball that got tighter and tighter until by midday I was literally doubled over in pain and could barely stand up straight.

This happened every day until I finally made some changes and quit that job. I just couldn't take it anymore; the stress was crippling me. The lingering effects of the damage that uncontrolled unrelenting stress did to my stomach, not for years, "just" for a few months, continue to affect me now decades later. Once done, the damage is never fully undone.

AAARGH!

CHRONIC STRESS – Grinding, Unrelenting, Most Debilitating*

*Anxiety, a typical reaction to stress, is debilitating when it becomes "an excessive, irrational dread of everyday situations", as defined by the NIMH, which reports that about 18% or 40 million US adults are affected by an anxiety disorder in any given year.

Serious symptoms of **chronic stress** include:

> **Impaired cognitive performance** (can't think clearly when stressed)

> **Sleep disruption** (trouble falling asleep and staying asleep)

> **Elevated blood pressure** (pounding heart)

> **Lowered immune function** (catch colds and other germs easily)

> **Slow wound healing** (due to impaired immune function)

> **Dampened thyroid function**

> ➢ **Blood sugar imbalances** (such as hypoglycemia)

> ➢ **Decreased bone density**

> ➢ **Decreased muscle mass**

> ➢ **Increased abdominal fat**

To highlight: ***chronic stress can kill brain cells, add fat, and unravel DNA*** – yikes! Let's avoid letting all three of those bad things happen.

Main SOURCES of Stress

- **Work, career**

- **Social, relationships**

- **Money, finances**

- **Physical, health issues**

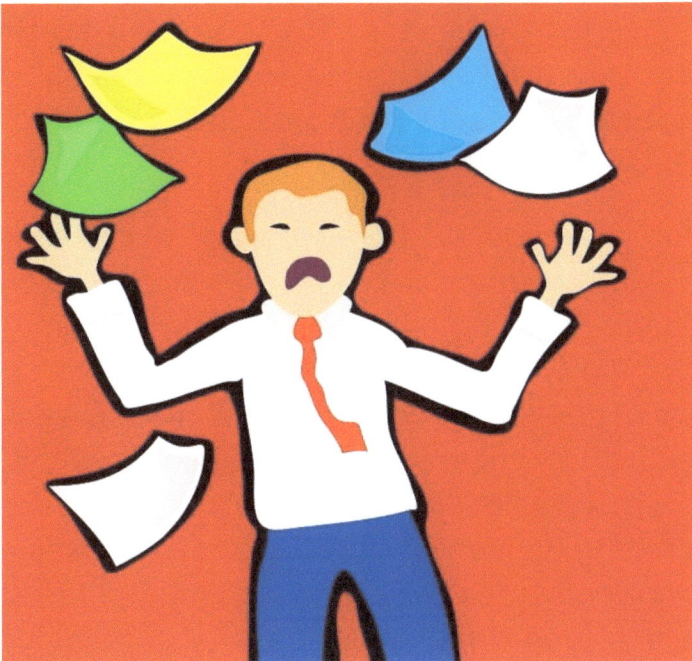

Your Job May Be *Killing You

We spend two thirds of our time at work including commuting. Workplace stress has tremendous and long-lasting health impact, and has a **direct link to heart disease, heart attacks, high blood pressure.**

According to the American Institute of Stress, **80% of workers feel stressed at work**, with nearly half of them reporting the need for help dealing with their stress.

The work stress experienced has **long-lasting negative health implications** as well as **negative impacts on home life relationships**.

Long work hours... bringing work stress home to those relationships (work stress causes poor behavior with friends and/or family at home)*... work/life balance issues... disengaged employees* (stressed employees have lower productivity, higher employer costs (healthcare expenditures nearly 50% greater for workers reporting high stress levels), and *increased absenteeism* (sick, plus taking "mental health days")*... job traveling is stressful... meeting deadlines... facing public scrutiny... dead-end, no growth potential... competitive work* *environment... physical job demands... environmental hazards on the job... life and/or responsibility for others' lives at risk... meeting the public...* ooooh, I have a stress headache just thinking about all of the negative impact!

"Could I see you in my office?"

"Oh, no..." you worry, *"what did he find to yell at me about I this time?"* There are so many possibilities, since you know that you do great work, but you admittedly also take some risks to get that good work done. As you muster up the courage to go in to see your tormentor, the fight or flight response kicks into high gear; the hypothalamus sends an urgent message to the adrenal glands – red alert! A high threat is imminent! Maybe you'd like to run and hide, or alternatively duke it out with the man, but you can't do either.

Meanwhile all the stress symptoms begin*: you start sweating with anxiety, your hands get clammy and wet, your heart starts racing, your blood is pounding through your veins, and as your mind races, you suddenly feel the urge to go to the bathroom.* You can't fight and you can't flee, so all the pent-up energy just builds up inside, with nowhere to go. You struggle to hold on to the explosive anxiety that is looking for an outlet to release, hoping you don't do or say something regrettable...

Overblown reaction or false alarm? It doesn't matter as the stress is real, as is the bodily response.

Job stress is impossible to eliminate 100% of the time. It is a part of working life, so it must be recognized, accepted as such, and handled appropriately.

Main Causes of Workplace Stress:
46% → heavy workload
28% → interpersonal relationships
20% → juggling work/life balance
6% → no job security

Most Stressful Jobs*
(*CareerCast.com, 2015 report)

High stress jobs require steely nerves to face unpredictable conditions, immediate dangers, and high-stakes situations. Those jobs that are the most stressful, physically and psychologically, require a certain personality type for success – absolutely not for everyone!

The 10 most stressful jobs are:

1. Firefighter (physical risk)

2. Enlisted Military (life at risk)

3. Military General (lives of others at risk)

4. Pilot (own life and lives of others at risk)

5. Police officer (own life at risk, protecting others)

6. Actor (public performing)

7. Broadcaster (public scrutiny)

8. Event coordinator (tight deadlines)

9. Photojournalist (personal safety getting the perfect shot)

10. Newspaper reporter (tight deadlines, public scrutiny)

Some people gravitate towards high stress jobs because for them, routine **stress is a**

motivator, they 'get off' on the adrenaline rush. But these people typically burn out fast and compromise their health if they don't learn how to control stress. Nature's plan was not for adrenaline to be repeatedly released in heavy prolonged doses.

In stressful workplaces and situations, the key factor to offset stress is **control** – when there is little control over the job pace or over job activities, health is negatively impacted. When people have control over the amount and types of stressors they encounter, they can do okay health-wise in high stress jobs for long periods of time without burning out.

Managing your emotions in times of stress allows you to remain calm and in control. However *prolonged stress causes degeneration in the prefrontal cortex where self-control comes from, making dealing with future stress even more challenging. (*Yale study)

Luckily the brain is very malleable and has the ability to be trained in healthy ways to deal with stress, like incorporating some of the 15 stress coping strategies included further on in this book.

Relationships are Critical for Affecting Good Health*

Reminding yourself of the important people in your life who you can count on – having social support – has the capacity to improve health and maintain it for longer periods of time.

"I'm seeing my family this weekend."

"If I need to, I can call my friend and talk over this problem."

Relationships serve as a buffer during tough times, improving cardiovascular functioning and decreasing stress levels.

Developing strong communication skills helps to strengthen relationships and avoid stressful misunderstandings with others.

Helping others, doing kind things for others, inoculates against stress.

*One study showed that an unfortunate side effect of being in a strained relationship was that it took almost twice as long for wounds to heal.

Financial Money Woes – The Top Stressor

When people live together, they share financial stress (or financial well-being). One household member's stress affects others in the same household, plus dealing with conflict on spending habits.

Is **financial security** intact: is there enough money to cover the basics?

Low financial well-being can lead to stress, anxiety, insomnia, headaches, depression, and poor relationships.

The two key areas pertaining to finance are:

> – What you do with your money

> - Your daily level of comfort/stress around money

Financial stress can take two different forms:

> → Stress caused by constant deprivation

> → Stress associated with success

Money doesn't alleviate stress like it alleviates unhappiness; money goes hand-in-hand with stress. You may be thinking, "Ha! I would love to have the stress of having too much money!" but the reality is you really wouldn't. Having too much money is its own burden, with its own distinct stressors.

Setting a realistic budget, with distinct parameters, helps mitigate the stress of going overboard (especially at the holidays) and keeping overspending in check.

Long-Term Stress Ruins Your Health

At the onset of stress, the brain grows new cells responsible for improved memory. But when stress continues beyond a few minutes into a prolonged state (chronic stress), it becomes debilitating, suppressing the brain's ability to generate new cells.

Modern brains have evolved in complexity, so now we can **worry and ruminate** on major and minor events, which causes frequent experiences of prolonged stress and false alarms – yikes! *What was THAT sound? Did you hear it? I'm sure there's something out there I should be worried about...*

Stress -

    - kills brain cells, decreases cognitive function → leads to memory loss

    - increases risk of heart disease → high blood pressure

    - contributes to anxiety, depression → loss of resiliency

    - contributes to obesity (insulin resistance) → adult diabetes correlation

Every time the body triggers the fight or flight response, with most events as not truly life-threatening, your body is experiencing a **false alarm.**

Repeated false alarms can lead to stress-related disorders:
- High blood pressure
- Heart disease
- Immune system disorders
- Migraines
- Insomnia
- Sexual dysfunction

What to do? Have a plan to deal with reducing routine stress before it gets out of hand. If stress is pretty constant and not released, it will do internal damage.

Also important is a belief that the plan to deal with problems in a non-stressful way will succeed. This greatly increases the likelihood of success.

One solution is to take vitamin B12 and zinc, which supports the immune system.

Also avoid eating trigger foods like coffee, eggs, and chocolate.

Stress Vulnerabilities

The usual suspects –
Diet (good diet, not "comfort" foods, which can make you feel worse)

Sleep (sleep deprivation lowers the tolerance for stress) and makes us more stress prone throughout the day

Exercise (cardiovascular exercise releases endorphins, making us feel happier and less stressed)

Smoking

Alcohol

Caffeine

Excess weight

And some others -
Social connections (regular socializing, talking - not just venting - with friends/coworkers can alleviate the pressure felt when stressed)

Deep relationships (emotional support and information/ideas from others helps to deal with stressors)

Ability to express emotions

Relaxation, having fun

Listening to music (soothing sounds like nature tracks or classical music can lower blood pressure after a stressful situation)

'Me' time

Daily commute

Ability to ask for help or a hug (releases calming oxytocin, which shuts down normal stress reaction)

Feeling of control (simplify life by limiting the stress of too many choices)

Using time well

Having enough money to cover the basics

Calm discussion of everyday problems (as a routine habit)

4 Options for Dealing with Stress

The Four Fs – when you realize you have a stressor in your life that's real and needs to be dealt with, Paul Coleman, author of *Finding Peace in Your Heart, When Your Heart is in Pieces*, outlines 4 'F' possible responses to deal with stress:

FIGHT: Anger/Blame drive this option

FLEE: Shut down or ignore the stressful situation

FOLD: Surrender or become helpless in the face of stress

FACE: Deal with the stressor head-on

The key is to deal with the stress once recognized, instead of falling into knee-jerk coping patterns that ultimately lead nowhere.

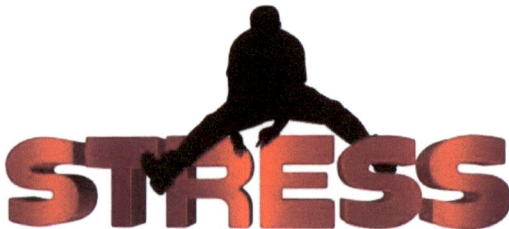

An Upside to Modern Stress...

Intermittent stress keeps the brain more alert, which **can enhance performance**.

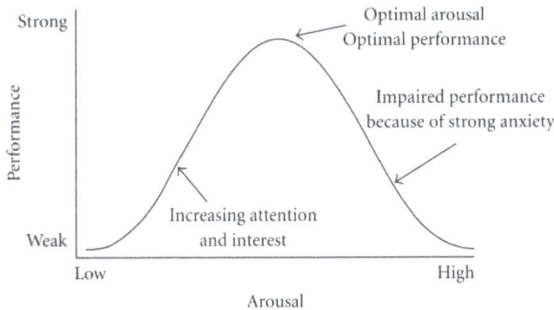

Making Stress Work in Your Favor

- Accept the fact that stress is part of life (*"I'm stressed out because I really care"*)

- Look for the message inside the stress reaction; what important thing are you avoiding that you need to do? (*"Why does this matter?"*)

- Allow the option of viewing the stress – the anger, the injustice, the error of your behavior – which can be a catalyst for something better

- Use the heightened state to perform better - while also remembering the importance of keeping stress under control!

Gender Differences

MEN   → have a more **aggressive response** to stress

→ tend to **withdraw socially** to cope with stress alone

→ are more likely to **abuse substances** to cope with stress

→ are overrepresented in homicides and suicides,

→ are overrepresented in alcoholics and drug abusers

The fight or flight pattern of coping with stress is potentially lethal for men.

WOMEN → are more likely to seek and give support in stressful situations

→ use the healthy stress responses of group tending /friending

→ live about 6 ½ years longer than men do

→ have better health, reduced risk of illness

The female stress-reduction strategy is healthier, therefore women enjoy a lower mortality than men.

15 Stress COPING STRATEGIES

Near constant tension of stress must be routinely released. Here are some ideas:

- Do your **least favorite** to-dos first

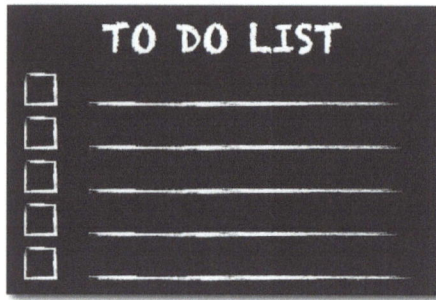

- **Laugh** (with others, co-workers), or at least think positive thoughts (like an exciting upcoming event to shift from negative to positive thoughts)

- Take a mid-day **break outside** (**disconnect from 24/7 technology** to keep stress intermittent instead of constant)

- **Focus on the present** (deep slow breaths floods the brain with oxygen, increasing the ability to think and react), or narrow your focus to the immediate future (zoom in on what's needed for just the next few minutes)

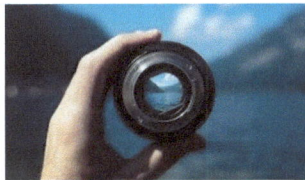

JUST BE

- **Avoid asking 'What if?' questions**, which just adds fuel to the stress and worry fire and take you places you don't need, or want, to go (worrying about possibilities takes time away from focusing on taking action and controlling stress)

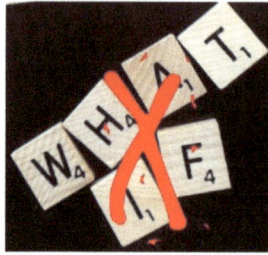

- **Eliminate negative self-talk** (stop ruminating negatively with thoughts that are just bad scenarios, not really facts)

- Maintain **positive beliefs** (i.e. hope, optimism), positive outlook

- **Reframe the perspective** (your anxiety may be out of proportion to reality)

- **Call on your support network** connections, use them regularly (ask for help to see a solution; don't go it alone with your worries)

- **Review the day's accomplishments** at the end of the day, and then **tell someone** about them (expressing gratitude, appreciation and accomplishment aloud improves mood, *reduces the stress hormone cortisol by 23% - *U Cal, Davis study)

- Really **relax during leisure time** (weekends, vacations)

- **Exercise** 2-5 days/week, in 30-minute time blocks

- Get good **sound sleep** at night, 7½ hours nightly is ideal (sleep increases EQ, recharges and clears the brain, to regain control and reduce stress)

- **Mindfulness meditation**, as short as 3 mins daily (focused relaxed breathing works wonders)

- **Smell some lavender** scent (calms and reduces stress)

Engage in rewarding work –

change jobs to find work you are passionate about – the best stress cure is work enjoyment!

A modern solution?

Here's a twist in our digital world of trying to combine the best of both worlds – work is the same as vacation with new concept of cabana offices.

Beach sites in exotic locations are renting cabanas as worksites equipped with wi-fi, electricity for charging, mini-fridges, and printing capability. With this setup a working parent can keep an eye and the kids while still being work productive. But still you have to wonder about the stress and tension of trying to maintain a dependable phone signal, power outages, and keeping technical equipment working properly in sand and surf, with a critical deadline pending.

There is a place for rest and relaxation, which is separate from the work environment. Can you really combine the two and do justice to both? Should you?

The SmartyPants Secret on STRESS

The one big cause for stress is the attaching of emotions to outcomes, or vice versa. By disengaging emotions from the outcomes of various activities can reduce stress levels.

Stress is a part of modern life; moderate stress and the accompanying anxiety are necessary emotions. We are wired to need some stress to feel the need to take action; we actually perform better with moderate levels of stress. When stress is intermittent, it is harmless.

The harm comes when stress is prolonged and chronic, without regular periods of relief. When stress becomes the rule instead of the exception, real internal bodily damage is done over time.

Ignoring the issue – denial – pretending it doesn't exist is a poor strategy, related to higher levels of stress. Like any major issue, stress needs to be recognized in order to be addressed and controlled, or it may indeed kill, with the severe internal damage that can result.

BOOK BUYER BONUS

As a thank you to buyers, there is an additional free resource available only to book buyers. Did you get yours? If you missed it, go to www.SmartyPantsSecrets.com/bookbonus .

It's has additional valuable content and is free to book buyers, so don't miss out on getting yours!

BOOK RESOURCE

This SmartyPants Secrets book has a companion resource on the topic that may be of interest. The resource for this Memory Book is a **100% natural organic *Herbal Blend De-STRESS Aid*, to support stress reduction.**

This ***Herbal Blend De-STRESS Aid*** not only works to support reducing stress organically, it also tastes great, and makes a caring gift for others you care about that may be experiencing their own stress issues.

For ordering and other information on this and

other SmartyPants Secrets support products, visit the website at www.SmartyPantsSecrets.com/resources

ABOUT

I am DR Martin, PhD* (*Personal human Development expertise) – Dolley Rapoport Martin. I took Dolley as my first name* in honor of the great First Lady Dolley Madison, whom I admire for her heroic actions in the White House during very turbulent times.

I took Rapoport as a middle name* in honor of Ingeborg Rapoport, who at age 103, is the oldest person to be awarded a Doctorate; finally getting the recognition due her from 77 years prior in Nazi Germany, unfairly denied her due to her Jewish roots. There is so much injustice in the world; it is an honor to recognize her achievement by taking her name. [*The selecting of one's name is an important exercise, since names are so personal and tied to identity. Yet most of us go through life with a name not of our choosing. Check out the SmartyPants Secret book NAMES.]

I have studied every communication subject for more than a decade, acquiring a large body of knowledge. I, perhaps like you, am a voracious reader and learner. My other strength is that I retain much of what I learn, so I can then compile the knowledge on a variety of subjects into a concise format, making the books that I author a shortcut on the best knowledge available. This saves you from going through all the data looking for the kernel that makes the greatest difference in success, the SmartyPants secret on a given topic.

I also have a mind that is ever curious about so many topics. I have earned multiple expert designations (education certified English teacher, Real Estate Broker, Stock Broker series 7, series 6, series, Certified Financial Manager, Insurance producer certified, Coach University) and held high level positions in business – large corporate entities, privately held companies, non-profit organizations, and startups – and have volunteered extensively, holding executive positions at the local, district and national levels. So I've been around the block more than once, on more than one topic.

Due to my research and experience, I have logged the perquisite time to carry the title of expert, giving myself an honorary PhD in the expertise area of communication, Personal human Development. I am passionate about sharing the knowledge that I have gained with you, in bite-size pieces.

And when a certain topic is not in my field of expertise, I find an expert with deep expertise in the field who has the knowledge that I seek. I then ask numerous in-depth questions of the expert to get to the gist, learn the SmartyPants Secret, to then pass the knowledge on in a book on the subject.

SMARTY**pants**
secrets

For other titles and additional resources, visit www.SmartyPantsSecrets.com

All book titles at www.amazon.com/-/e/B018HA35I8

Watch for content clips and helpful technique tips on a variety of topics coming soon at www.youtube.com/c/smartypantssecrets

Contact: Info@SmartyPantsSecrets.com

9 7 8 1 9 4 3 9 7 1 1 4 5